If You're Reading This, I Have Some
Questions

A Collection of Poems

By Rebecca Routh-Sample

Published by Lulu Press 2025

ISBN 978-1-326-31757-7

Published 2025 by Lulu Press Inc

Other books by Rebecca Routh-Sample

Fiction

Diary Of A Teenage Fangirl

Diary Of A Teenage Rebel Girl

In Real Life

Poetry

Ghost World

Donnie Darko

Paramour

Spinner's End

The Greatest Love Story Never Told

Maybe You Never Loved Me As Much As You Loved New York

If You're Reading This, I Have Some Questions

All available to purchase on

www.lulu.com

Connect with me on social media if you want! I'd love to hear your feedback:

Twitter: @itsbeccafy

Instagram: @beccafyofficial

TikTok: @itsbeccafy

Contents

If You're Reading This, I Have Some Questions

What makes you think you can hurt her, and I'd just let it go?

We may not be the best of friends, but she's a person I know

Rapists, murderers, abusers

They can all go to hell

No time, no words

I don't want to hear it

No explanations, no excuses

I don't want to hear it

I don't want to hear your side of the story

I want to hear her side of the story

I have nothing to say to you

Not a single thing

Pull up a chair

And start bloody listening

Don't You Want To Hear My Side Of The
Story?

Welcome to my hurt locker

The evidence is sealed

The case is

Odd Child VS. The People

The charges are

I have bad taste in men

I have bad taste in friends

My judgement is clouded

By the chemicals in my head

There's overwhelming evidence

The names are redacted

But there's three with four letters

They're almost an anagram

The specifics will only be

picked up by the true fans

The jury of my peers

Are cynical as hell

They know the wealth of information

The internet and newspapers

The secrets

They have held

Over these tracks

They will be telled

Let's call our first defendant...

But don't you want to hear
My side of the story
The blood evidence
The DNA it's gory

Three criminals on the stand
The misogynistic actor
The car crash lover
And the most angelic man
Whose sole crime
Was never loving me back

A predator
A criminal

A menace to society

A drug user

A danger

Really bad at comedy

A cannibal

A con-man

A mutant

A ghost

A cult leader

Running

faster than the speed

of light

Crashing

into doll

houses

Don't you want to hear my side of the story?

Don't you

Don't you

Don't you

I Know What You Crave

Pop a melatonin

Sleep on me

But I know what you crave

And you're nuts

if you think this is a publicity stunt

I loved a man that wasn't

a man or even a boy

He was a figment of my

imagination

In the island of misfit toys

He was on a different

metaphysical plane

That's funny if he's just an idea

He caused a lot of literal material pain

And a lesser person would have

been driven completely insane

But I think that people forget my

name

I'm addicted to the updates

Notifications of disaster

Twitter blasts and storms

You can't cover with plasters

When you're terminally online

Drama is your master

Variety is a slice of life

Vanity is always fair

Paper cut my fingers

Pitchfork in the back

PageSix, the Demon's holy bible

Bittersweet at

Seventeen because

I'm your teen idol

Pop a melatonin

Sleep on me

But I know what you crave

Back From The Edge

I have to live life

Looking out a window

With people thinking

I was the one that hurt you

I have to live with

people critiquing my tweets

Even if they were true

Leaving that hotel room

Scars on me

And scars on you

And your husband

whose sobriety fell off the

minute he met you

I hold my girl's hand tighter

I don't want to remember

being burned by

your cigarette lighter

I hope the memory hurts you

Remember what happened

In that house on the hill

The creepy dolls

and bad actors

Ghosts, halloween masks,

clowns, all the factors

That drove me to the edge

Until she saved my life

Pulled me back again

Back from the edge

I have to live counting my blessings

He ghosted me when he did

No morals, no opinions

And his looks were just mid

Dating a bad actor, fake lawyer,

school bully, bad mother

Glad I got away from that

Glad I'm not the brand that

was branded

In the California fakeness

In a Bel Air mansion

Honesty is my passion

I'm glad I missed that Saturday night

I'm so glad I missed that Saturday night

I was alone

With my broken bones

Until he saved my life

Pulled me back again

Right from the edge

I swear I'd give my life

to have her dead

I swear I'd give my life

to save yours instead

Let's put it to bed

As lies next to me

Sweetly

in my bed

The Real Thing

She's not a feminist

Or an anarchist

But in your eyes

I guess

That's a positive

I spend nights working

on my craft

While she does the opposite

Create new insecurities

Spread them like Halloween Candy

sharp or sweet

and find a way to

profit it off them easily

All she ever talks about is

who she knows

and where she's going

With her yes men

And fair-weather friends

And the newest trends

But I don't care about

Who you know and

How you know them

I don't care about where

you go

And how you flew there

So I just hang out
with my real friends
I don't care
about passing trends
I don't do it for the 'gram
I don't do it for my man
I do what is the right thing
The good thing
The real thing

So I just hang out
with my real friends
I don't care
about passing trends
I don't do it for the 'gram

I might just do it for my man

Because he is the right thing

The good thing

The real thing

If I Was A Smart Girl

If I ever lost you

I'd kill myself Romeo and Juliet style

No questions

And if a bitch trifles you

I'll be in their mentions

If I was a smart girl

I'd learn my lesson

I would've never practised

with a partner that never wanted to

dance

You took my young years, my youth and
my fertility

And diagnosed my apathy

As comorbidity

To your fatal diagnosis of

being too much for simply being me

And you prescribed a lobotomy

And a dose of trad wife to tackle my 4B

Movement in my face

I can still gurn

I can still hiss

I can still take a gun

And hold it to your lips

I could kill you in your sleep

And get away with it

And if they fry me it'll be worth it

I'd rather electric chair

Than electro convulsive therapy

On my own terms

Not in this messed up

Paradox it seems

The only way to survive is

to pick a different team

If I was a smart girl

I could have differentiated

a nightmare

from a dream

Night Light

You have this remarkable power

To stop me dead in my tracks

Talk on the phone for hours

In the night time there's a garden

where you wait for me

You're in of all my daydreams

You never back down

We simply lay under the stars

You are my future, present,

forever, always, everywhere

You're safety, light and comfort

You're never not there

In the beginning of time

In the apocalypse

I wished upon a falling star

You landed right into my heart

Sleepover tonight

You can be my night light

Because when I turn the lights off

You're still so bright

Stay with me baby

Lay here all night

I won't be scared of the dark

You're my night light

Daniel

Tell me your biggest secret

Daniel

I looked at it from every angle

I just don't know

What are my intentions?

I'm in your mentions

I don't know

It's Tuesday night

Why don't you give me a call?

I can see you now

It's 9pm and I'm not heading out

I revered you

I admired you so

Eclipsed by something greater

Long nights in a trailer

Was the ground covered in snow?

In my restless dreams

You were my foundational trauma

You were my achilles heal

My first, forever, former

And we lost touch

God knows why

We were brother and sister

In another life

I wanted to be you
I wanted to help you
I'm happy you're healing now
It was a really long night
and I'm glad you made it out

I'll see you now
9pm
Tuesday night

Eclipse

You were there by my side

Trapped in this prison of lies

It was my own making

If I didn't have armour

I wouldn't make it through the

night

Exorcise my soul, my mind, my body

Take the sunlight from my soul

Be that parasocial emblem

That thing I shoot in my veins

When life feels wrong

I was a hostage to my expectations

Set fire to all my clothes

I'm becoming a new person tomorrow

You have eclipsed my soul

You were that idol I
worshipped all day long
Redemption

There is no room for redemption
For someone like you
There is no room for mercy
If there's no room for truth
Don't forget what they did to you
If they look at you with a match
Ready to light the gas
As if to say 'Don't do that, I'll bury you
and I tell them you're crazy too'
You cannot give that man an inch

You cannot laugh or smile

Look look at him with eyes that say

'I know exactly

what you did motherfucker

and Jesus knows that too

You can recite the words

But it doesn't make them true

You can twist parables with pervesity

And become the

pastor of fake news

But it doesn't make the truth any less true'

Grab her hand as if to say

'I know what he did to you

even if he didn't do it to me too'

Solidarity is the only antidote

to corruption

And you know it deep in your soul

Don't settle being the wife of a Shepard

No matter if your stockings

are full of coal or gold

It doesn't matter

Don't present your intelligence

and compliance on a silver platter

To be devoured by a being with

no soul

Eat up the meat, spit out the bones

Run, girl

Even if you're not young, girl

Sometimes the devil
looks like an angel when he
smiles at you
Sometimes God tests us by
presenting everything you want
on a silver platter
but you know deep down it's not true
It's fallacy and fiction
An actor with a porn addiction
As many allegations and
condemnations
As badly pressed suits
and ugly cowboy boots

Death by Heartbreak / Love's Labours Lost

I've been in love with you since the first time I saw you

On my television screen

Couldn't forget your smile

Imprinted in my memory

And ever since then I've been sitting my window

Hoping, praying for you to come home

I waited all this time

I've never met you, my only friend

But I'd wait a million lifetimes all over again

Absence makes the heart grow fonder

But if I have to wait any longer

I'll surely end up dead

Susie Salmon

So you didn't come to my birthday and
you're harassing me still

7 years of it eating away at you and you
still haven't had your fill

Call me Susie Salmon

I'll haunt every dream

Every icicle has a reflection of me

refract and break the ice

180 degrees

Waving from your snow globe

You'll never be at peace

It's my party, Sally

I'll cry if I want to

Simon says that what Sally says about
Susie says more about Sally then it does
of Susie

but I think Sally's full of shit

she's full of it

and I'm going to make sure

you'll never be at peace

Impossible Girl

Do you see me

like a girl trapped in a tower?

Rapunzel, Marianne,

Kathy or Jane?

Do you think of me

like some fixed point in time?

I'll never grow

Never change

Never older

Just the same

Perpetual

Teenage days

I'm a human living girl

I want to be out there in

the world

Not a myth

Urban legend

Never destroyed

Never taken

Do you think you

are the catalyst of

my time line?

I want a life without you

I want to walk on the land

like human beings do?

I'm not a daydream

Sleeping Beauty

I'm the queen

If you want an Impossible Girl

Carve her out of stone

Because she isn't me

We had something

History textbooks

Can't understand

The sweetest boy

he was holding my hand

I treated him like trash

So he set sail to conquer

a new world

Left me to drown

In the sink

Like leftover coffee

Too much liquor

On the brink

Leaving some alone

to cure their loneliness?

I went crazy

What do did you think?

And I never saw

Anything bad in you

And I never saw

Those facts

Categorically true

Shame I'm a smart girl

I can twist my brain into

a loop

Make my life all about you

So what's your excuse?

That stupid box

That garden shed

Who are you?

To tell me how, where

and when?

Some friend

The only thing worth

anything is time

I was spent

Up trying to pretend

I'm not an Impossible Girl

I made you my whole world

And I'm taking my subtle knife

And I'm off somewhere else

Pretty Girl

Pretty girl

What a shame you got such an ugly soul

Spouting therapist mind tricks

but we know

Privilege and euro-centric beauty is the

cheat code

And there isn't anyone you don't know

And you texting them on the low

Carrying your boyfriend in tow

Pinky promises and child support

Won't fix the lives you broke

And you ain't ever ever

gonna be broke

Family wealth and that blood runs slow

Delusions of grandeur thinking you're
the goat

Sneaky manager got that

echo-chamber saying 'Dope'

Friends, you mean yes men

that do what they're told?

How do you got so much sleep

with the demons at your throat?

He's your soulmate?

That's a big cope

You treated him like trash

Went for another man

Then he's gone and

you abandon that other man

They wallpaper over

with a paper and a pencil

and a trace

Then the doppelgänger

Took as much as he could take

Then you cheated on him

With a so-called family man

Where does it end?

Do you really have any true

friends?

Anyone to address you with contempt?

To wash it over, yeah shit

I did some fucked up shit

Maybe it's time to repent?

Stuck up in the clouds

get on planet Earth

Think about to 'live an authentic life'

How many people you put in the dirt

I don't know man I'm just

a person

with moral and standards

and a conscience and accountability

and real people around me

but they don't orbit around me

He's a family man?

Then where's his family at

If he's a family man

Where his family at?

So I Called Ashley

So I called Ashley

I told her about you and I

I was just in my feelings

Then she gives me the biggest surprise

'I can forgive, I can forget

I almost died so I meant what I said

Everyone deserves a second chance

I want to see you happy again'

So we went out for ice cream

You, she, her lover, and me

We it buried it all

Along with our hatches

Held hands and sauntered away

But vipers with cameras

and bad intentions

Their poison ivy enveloped me

like weeds

'If this really is the end of all ends

why do I feel so free?'

Because I've got to a place

where I don't care about

what people think of me

Except to the closest to me

And that's why I called Ashley

And she said

'That's all that matters to me'

Car Crash

You were such a car crash

But you know what baby

I loved that

We met in the strangest of ways

We met on the strangest of days

There were people all around us

But all I could see was your face

NEW YORK

Saturday night

Serendipity

The red ribbon

Our hands were tied

Baby, baby,

Burn off the tattoos

In that Razor Light

Drink some Hennessy

And chase it down

Like a suburban L.A. night

Underwater I was drowning

Thank God you found me

Human Race

Just because you can quote the sermon
doesn't mean you have all the answers

Just because you move quick

doesn't mean you run faster

And just because it's fast

doesn't mean it's a disaster

And just because you have a lot of money

it doesn't make it your master

I've spent a long time
Running away from my self
Too much self-indulgence
And not enough professional help
And I've seen many a man
make the mistake as well
That we are naked as the day we're born
And are destined to go straight to hell

Down To Earth

It was like my life began

When you fell down from the sky
I only saw in black and white
But you're a physical manifestation
of a rainbow
I'll admit I was really boring
Not a single thing in life sorted
'How to love' it's like you taught it
Sold me happiness
and I bought it
Now I'm obsessed with everything you
do

Taught me how to be human
Taught me love
Now I can master my emotions
Your music and my thoughts

I owe you everything of course

My life started on
That day you fell down to Earth

Shoot Your Star

I'll admit
that I fell in love
with him
about the same time
she fell in love with him
she was newly divorced
and she needed a win
I'd do anything to be with him

she was his prize

I was a ritual sacrifice

I was the best thing since

sliced bread

chasing those highs

you need to come back home

let me be the Forrest

to your Jenny

I'll be waiting on my front porch

bat for you

hold your torch

light Babylon candles

and wish on a shooting star

like airplanes in the night sky

sky high before your drive by

don't shoot your star

don't let your light fade out

don't let the rain drown you

don't let your tears confound you

don't let jokers mess with the king

don't worry if your haters try you

'cause they're bound to

but let your friends be around you

remind you

just how loved you are

a heart's a heavy burden

but I'll hold it in a heartbeat

let it hurt me

let it curse me

forever into the depths

of the waste and the burdens

of being

a living human girl

out there in the world

permission of the author. Brief
quotations are okay in review.

ISBN 978-1-326-31757-7

Published 2025 by Lulu Press Inc

9 781326 317577

www.ingramcontent.com/pod-product-compliance
Ingram Content Group UK Ltd.
Pitfield, Milton Keynes, MK11 3LW, UK
UKHW020111091125
8818UKWH00021B/473